THE RITTEROO *Journal*

for eating disorders recovery

LINDSEY HALL

Foreword by Carolyn Costin
Artwork by Mary Anne Ritter
Design by Francesca Droll

gürze books

The Ritteroo Journal for Eating Disorders Recovery

Gürze Books
P.O. Box 2238
Carlsbad, CA 92018
760-434-7533
gurzebooks.com

ISBN-13: 978-0-936077-77-2 (trade paperback)

NOTE:
The author and publisher of this book intend for this journal to complement,
not substitute for, professional medical and/or psychological services.

Printed in the United States of America
1 3 5 7 9 0 8 6 4 2

TABLE OF CONTENTS

DEDICATION

Mary Anne Ritter (aka "Ritteroo") was a talented graphic designer, seminar leader, and career coach who also had an eating disorder. In the summer of 2002, she sent preliminary artwork and designs for an eating disorder journal to me at Gürze Books, hoping to get it published. I was enthusiastic about the project, and we were several months into the editing process together when Mary Anne unexpectedly passed away, and it was shelved.

I always wanted to honor Mary Anne's legacy by fulfilling her dream of a journal specific to eating disorder recovery, but somehow, the time never seemed right. Making matters more difficult, all I had was a single copy of the manuscript and some laminated cards of her artwork—no computer files or images saved on disc. Still, every time I would pull her pages off the shelf, the ideas and designs remained as inspiring, beautiful, and relevant as ever.

More than ten years have passed since Mary Anne left us, and for reasons I can't really explain, *now* feels like the right time to offer her gifts to everyone. From her estate, I have collected more samples of her artwork, which our graphic designer, Francesca Droll, has been able to work with and replicate beautifully. Along with her art, I have taken the liberty of organizing, editing, and supplementing her journal prompts and affirmations into a book that I hope honors her memory and vision in the best possible way.

—Lindsey Hall

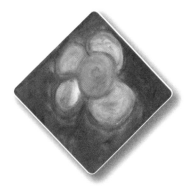

FOREWORD

I discovered the magical power of journaling many years ago, when I was first overcoming my eating disorder. At the time, I didn't know why putting my thoughts down on paper helped me—or even how much it contributed to my recovery—but somehow it made me feel better. When I became a therapist in the late 1970s, I began encouraging my clients to make daily journal entries…and still do today.

Research shows that journal writing integrates the right and left hemispheres of the brain and calms down emotional reactivity. A survey of my eating disorder clients showed that the three most important contributions to their recovery were journaling, not weighing themselves, and reaching out for support at the first sign of a problem. I tell all my clients and you the reader: since almost everyone in my practice who recovered did those three things, you should try doing them, too!

This beautiful *Ritteroo Journal for Eating Disorders Recovery* will make the journaling process easier and more enjoyable for you.

Lindsey Hall, a dear friend who also recovered from an eating disorder around the same time that I did, organized this project and brought it to life. Ten years ago, she and Mary Anne Ritter, a brilliant artist in recovery, had begun working on it together when Mary Anne passed away unexpectedly. Recently, Lindsey and I were looking through the original artwork, which I inherited—and the journal was reborn.

We've dedicated this book to Mary Anne, who not only provided the artwork, but the inspiration, as well. She dreamed of touching others through her creativity and does it beautifully here on these pages. In her memory, a percentage of proceeds will be donated to non-profit organizations devoted to eating disorders recovery.

The use of journals and writing to discover one's inner secrets and give voice to one's soul had a profound and lasting impact on my recovery. I can no longer remember a time when writing didn't occupy a part of my day. It is my hope that this journal workbook will provide a safe space in which each of you can discover your voice and put words to your challenges, triumphs, and dreams.

—Carolyn Costin

My Relationships

"An eating disorder cannot take
the place of true friendships.
It cannot protect you or
make you feel good about yourself.
Nor can it fill that empty place inside you.
And when you take the courageous step
to cut ties with your disorder,
you will learn, as I did, that

*there is nothing
more nurturing or fulfilling
than a relationship
based on honest sharing,
mutual respect, and true self-love.*"

REBECCA COOPER

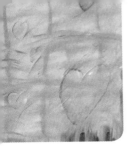

When I find myself feeling isolated and alone,
here are the reasons why I should connect with other people:

_____
_____
_____
_____
_____
_____
_____
_____
_____
_____
_____
_____
_____
_____
_____
_____
_____
_____
_____
_____
_____
_____
_____
_____
_____
_____
_____
_____
_____
_____
_____

_"Each friend
represents a world in
us, a world possibly not
born until they arrive, and
it is only by this meeting
that a new world
is born."_

ANAIS NIN

My Relationships

The help I need is out there and I will take these steps to find it:

_____

_____

_____

_____

_____

_____

_____

_____

_____

_____

_____

_____

_____

_____

_____

_____

_____

_____

_____

_____

_____

_____

_____

_____

*"It takes two
to speak the truth:
one to speak, and
another to hear."*

HENRY DAVID
THOREAU

THIS IS WHAT
A PROFESSIONAL
COULD HELP ME WITH:

Therapist:

Nutritionist or dietician:

Medical doctor:

Psychiatrist:

Other:

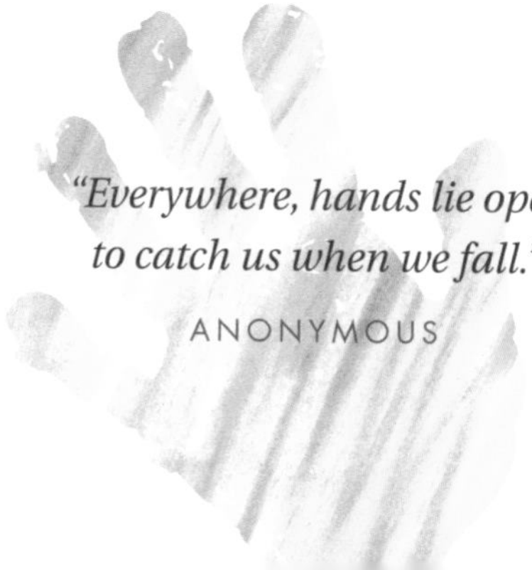

*"Everywhere, hands lie open
to catch us when we fall."*
ANONYMOUS

My Relationships

WHEN I FEEL SCARED, I KNOW I CAN
REACH OUT AND ASK FOR
HELP AND SUPPORT.

IN THIS WAY, I WILL BE
true to my feelings
AND
myself today.

This is what I might say when I talk to someone about my eating disorder:

_____

_____

_____

_____

_____

_____

_____

_____

_____

_____

_____

_____

_____

_____

_____

_____

_____

_____

_____

_____

_____

_____

_____

_____

_____

_____

A *Letter* TO ED

Write a goodbye letter to your eating disorder here:

_____

_____

_____

_____

_____

_____

_____

_____

_____

_____

_____

_____

_____

_____

_____

_____

_____

_____

_____

_____

_____

_____

Sometimes, taking care of myself means learning to say "no" when that reflects what I truly want or believe. Here are different ways I can say no:

❋ *That may be okay with you, but it's not okay with me.*

❋ *That's not my job, but I'd be willing to help.*

❋ *I know we disagree about this issue, and that's okay.*

❋ *Let me get back to you with an answer.*

Add your own…

I HAVE THE
Right
TO SET LIMITS
AND THE COURAGE
TO DO SO.

*"Someone seeking freedom
from disordered eating must
maintain a balance between her
need to be in relationships with others
and her need to remain true to herself."*

ANITA JOHNSTON

Today, I am taking time alone for quiet reflection
in order to hear the beauty of my own song.

TODAY,
I will TRUST myself to know
what I need to CARE for myself, and
to know when to ask for HELP in my journey.

WRITE A DESCRIPTION
OF YOURSELF
FROM THE POINT OF VIEW
OF SOMEONE
WHO KNOWS YOU WELL.

I have the courage
TO LISTEN
TO OTHERS
even when it is
difficult or scary.

People

I CAN COUNT ON
NO MATTER WHAT

My Thoughts

"Gratitude

unlocks the fullness of life.
It turns what we have into enough,
and more. It turns denial into accep-
tance, chaos to order, confusion to clarity.
It can turn a meal into a feast, a house into
a home, a stranger into a friend. Gratitude
makes sense of our past, brings peace
for today and creates a vision
for tomorrow."

MELODY BEATTIE

Here is a list of everything that I'm grateful for,
whether small or large, in the past or present,
tangible or intangible, to remind me that

I am capable of feeling joy and hope.

> "Earth's
> crammed
> with heaven"
>
> ELIZABETH
> BARRETT
> BROWNING

CHALLENGE
SOME OF YOUR
AUTOMATIC ED THOUGHTS
BY ASKING...

Is that thought true?

How do I react when I believe this thought?

Can I react a different way or change my belief?

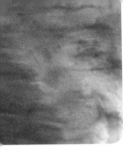

I CHOOSE TO THINK
healing, loving, AND thankful thoughts.

It is only
our own mind
that needs to be healed.

A COURSE IN MIRACLES

I HAVE THE

Courage

TO MAKE
MY MIND
MY FRIEND

My Thoughts

"IF ONE IS LUCKY, *a solitary fantasy* CAN TOTALLY TRANSFORM A MILLION REALITIES."

MAYA ANGELOU

My deepest wish for today is:

_____
_____
_____
_____
_____
_____
_____
_____
_____
_____
_____
_____
_____
_____
_____
_____
_____
_____
_____
_____
_____
_____
_____
_____

Positive Affirmations

Affirmations are positive thoughts that you repeat
to yourself to challenge and transform the negative
self-talk that can dominate your inner conversations.
Affirmations should have personal significance,
for example:

✴ *I am doing the best I can right now and that is enough.*
✴ *I deserve to eat, live, laugh, and love completely!*
✴ *Each day I grow stronger in my recovery.*

Here is my list of positive affirmations:

HERE ARE SOME OF MY FAVORITE
Quotes, Mantras, and Ideas.

I trust in the perfection of the present moment.

"**Mindfulness** is the practice of becoming aware of the present moment without judgment. Mindfulness separates you from your eating disorder by making you a witness to the unfolding of your thoughts and emotions—less critical, more accepting—and therefore increasingly present to the richness of everyday life."

LINDSEY HALL

Creating
A SAFE PLACE
FOR ME

As you make your journey through recovery and begin to leave old, dysfunctional behaviors behind, you may, at times, feel unsteady or unsure. Creating a "safe place" in your mind can be tremendously helpful and comforting. This safe place becomes a sacred retreat in which you feel protected, secure, and in control of your surroundings, feelings, and emotions. Your safe place might be a real physical location, (a dune on a favorite beach or a particular spot of grass near a special pond), an activity that you imagine doing (riding a horse or swinging on a swing) or even an imaginary place that you create in your mind. The main purpose of this "safe place" is that it gives you feelings of security and protection.

Here is a description of my very own safe place:

_____

_____

_____

_____

_____

_____

_____

_____

_____

_____

_____

_____

_____

_____

_____

_____

_____

_____

_____

_____

_____

_____

_____

_____

_____

_____

_____

_____

_____

_____

Values

A GOAL is a target—something that can be crossed off a list, an action item, like "eat one fear food this week."

VALUES, on the other hand, are basic principles that guide your goals, like "being flexible about my eating."

GOALS are what you want to do, VALUES are how you want to do them. Examples of values are generosity, honesty, and friendship.

This is a list of some of the things I value:
(Rate each one on a scale of 1 to 10 as to the degree you are living in accordance with these values. How might you improve that score?)

_____

_____

_____

_____

_____

_____

_____

_____

_____

Goals

What do I want to do with my life 3 months from now?

_____

_____

_____

_____

_____

_____

_____

_____

_____

_____

_____

_____

_____

_____

_____

_____

_____

_____

_____

_____

What do I want to do with my life 1 year from now?

_____

_____

_____

_____

_____

_____

_____

_____

_____

_____

_____

_____

_____

_____

_____

_____

_____

_____

_____

_____

_____

_____

_____

_____

_____

What do I want to do with my life 5 years from now?

_____

_____

_____

_____

_____

_____

_____

_____

_____

_____

_____

_____

_____

_____

_____

_____

_____

_____

_____

_____

_____

_____

_____

"Whatever you can do or dream you can do, begin it. BOLDNESS *has genius, power and magic in it."*

GOETHE

_____

_____

_____

_____

What do I want to be able to say to myself when I look back on this time in my life?

THE *Mind* IS LIKE A FERTILE FIELD.

WHATEVER *You*

PLANT AND CULTIVATE WILL BEAR FRUIT.

****** * ******
¡¡¡¡¡¡ FRIENDSHIP ¡¡¡¡¡¡¡
**** * ********
¡¡¡¡ GENEROSITY ¡¡¡¡¡¡¡¡
*********** * ****
¡¡¡¡¡¡¡¡¡¡¡¡ KINDNESS ¡¡¡¡
** *************
¡¡ COURAGE ¡¡¡¡¡¡¡¡¡¡¡¡¡
****** ********
¡¡¡¡¡¡¡ HONESTY ¡¡¡¡¡¡¡¡
***** ***
¡¡¡¡¡¡¡ TRUSTING OTHERS ¡¡¡
** * *****
¡¡ EXPRESSING FEELINGS ¡¡¡¡¡

What would I like to plant today?

My Feelings

"FEELINGS

connect us to our internal world, much like the senses connect us to the outside world. They are not something to avoid, but something to value—messages from an internal guidance system that fights for who you are and what you need as a person."

LINDSEY HALL

I will HONOR and VALUE my feelings, and
be attentive to what they are teaching me.
This is what I am feeling today:

> *"The irony is that if you give them half a chance, your deepest heartaches might just pave the way to your greatest happiness."*
>
> KAREN KOENIG

It is not the feelings themselves that cause disordered eating or an obsession with food. It is an attempt not to feel the feelings, or to handle them by abusing food.

In what situations am I able to trust my feelings and take chances?

"Never apologize for
*showing
your feelings.*
When you do,
you are apologizing
for the TRUTH."

JOSÉ N. HARRIS

My Feelings

EACH DAY I AM
MORE AWARE OF
my feelings
AND EXPRESS THEM
EASILY AND *lovingly.*

"Feelings come and go
like clouds in a windy sky.
Conscious breathing is my anchor."

THICH NHAT HAHN

One of the GREAT STEPS IN RECOVERY involves learning to have your feelings, but not be ruled by them.

My Feelings

Emotions

I CAN OBSERVE
MY FEELINGS,
WITHOUT JUDGMENT
OR THE DESIRE TO
CHANGE THEM.

RECOGNIZING MY EMOTIONS

The following is a list of emotions. Circle the ones you know you've experienced before, underline the emotions you can identify with now.

abandoned	cranky	exposed	irritated	proud
accepted	crazy	frightened	isolated	sad
affectionate	crushed	foolish	jealous	shy
alone	curious	frantic	joyful	sorry
aloof	defeated	friendly	kind	strong
amused	deflated	fulfilled	lazy	surprised
angry	dejected	full	loyal	terrified
annoyed	delighted	furious	lucky	tolerant
anxious	dependent	generous	lonely	troubled
apologetic	depressed	glad	listless	trusting
ashamed	desirable	grateful	mad	unappreciated
aware	desperate	grumpy	mean	unaware
betrayed	devastated	guilty	miserable	uncertain
bitter	disgusted	happy	negative	understood
bored	different	helpless	naughty	upset
brave	disappointed	hopeless	needy	useless
calm	discouraged	humiliated	nervous	valued
capable	dejected	hurt	nice	victimized
caring	distracted	hopeful	optimistic	violated
cautious	distressed	impatient	overwhelmed	vulnerable
cheerful	dominated	inadequate	paranoid	weary
confident	eager	incompetent	patient	wary
confused	ecstatic	indignant	purposeful	wiped out
composed	elated	innocent	powerful	wonderful
conflicted	embarrassed	insecure	peaceful	wounded
connected	enraged	interested	pleased	withdrawn
content	envious	irate	powerless	worthwhile
courageous	excited	irked	preoccupied	

My Feelings

EXPRESSING MY EMOTIONS

Think over the day and make a list of all the emotions you can recall feeling. Then, write about the emotions you let yourself express as well as those you resisted.

What did you notice?

"When I write, I make discoveries about my feelings."

write

GAIL CARSON
LEVINE

"ANGER

can bring clarity and strength.

A good relationship with our angry feelings can give us the determination to forge ahead, the strength to 'stand our own ground,' the energy and focus to let the world around us know what is and is not okay."

ANITA JOHNSTON

I give myself permission to blow up constructively!

This is what ticks me off:

This is why:

This is how I need things to be different:

I LET GO OF
FEELINGS
THAT ARE NOT MINE.

_____
_____
_____
_____
_____
_____
_____
_____
_____
_____
_____
_____
_____
_____
_____
_____
_____
_____
_____
_____
_____
_____
_____

**I HAVE THE
COURAGE**
*to allow others
to take responsibility
for themselves.*

"THERE IS NOTHING WRONG WITH
crying.
YOUR FEELINGS TELL YOU WHO YOU ARE.
THEY TELL WHAT IS IMPORTANT.
DON'T EVER BE ASHAMED OF THEM."

TERRY BROOKS

I have a right to my feelings, whatever they are.

"W⬡NDER

is a bulky emotion.
When it fills your heart and mind
there is little room for anything else."

DIANE ACKERMAN

Today I am amazed by:

_____

_____

_____

_____

_____

_____

_____

_____

_____

_____

_____

_____

_____

_____

_____

_____

_____

_____

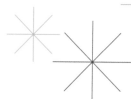

My Feelings

Courage

I AM PROUD OF MYSELF
WHEN I DARE TO RISK.

I have the courage to face my fear of:

_____

_____

_____

_____

_____

_____

_____

_____

_____

_____

_____

_____

_____

_____

_____

_____

_____

_____

_____

_____

_____

*"The best
way out
is always
through."*

ROBERT
FROST

*"The best and
most beautiful things
cannot be seen or even touched,
they must be felt within
the heart."*

HELEN KELLER

What is in my heart today?

My Heart

Extra Ora

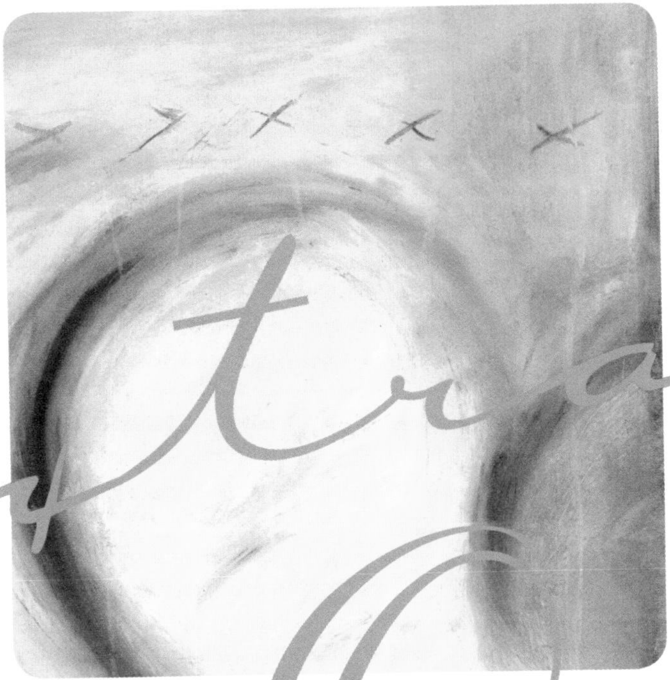

★

*"Maybe one
of these days I'll be
able to give myself a gold star
for being ordinary, and maybe one
of these days I'll give myself a gold star
for being extraordinary—for
persisting. And maybe one
day I won't need a
star at all."*

SUE BENDER

★

My Heart

TODAY,

I am FREE TO CREATE
that which makes me happy,
which is:

create

"The work of
ART
I do not make,
none other will ever make it."

SIMONE WEIL

Life Lessons

Make a timeline of your life in increments,
using school years or significant events as dividers.

My timeline:

Can you describe the lessons you learn in each?

_____

_____

_____

_____

_____

_____

_____

_____

_____

_____

How are those lessons serving you now?

" The *most exhausting* thing you can do is be *inauthentic.* "

ANNE MORROW LINDBERGH

Today I will be honest, express my truth, and take up space in the world.

My Heart

Exploring
SELF-ESTEEM

What are the positive things I associate with being me?

_____
_____
_____
_____
_____
_____
_____
_____
_____
_____
_____
_____
_____
_____
_____
_____
_____
_____
_____
_____
_____
_____
_____
_____
_____
_____

The things I feel competent in are:

_____

_____

_____

_____

_____

_____

_____

_____

_____

_____

What I value most about myself is:

_____

_____

_____

_____

_____

_____

_____

_____

_____

_____

_____

The things I feel most passionate about are:

HERE AND NOW

I celebrate myself

AND THE WAYS THAT I AM
OUTSTANDING, UNIQUE,
AND PRECIOUS.

What I like most about myself is:

_____

_____

_____

_____

_____

_____

_____

_____

_____

_____

The things that make me unique are:

_____

_____

_____

_____

_____

_____

_____

_____

_____

_____

_____

WEIGHTY *Matters*

What do "thin" and "fat" mean to me?

When did I first use my weight to reflect my self-esteem?

What do I think will happen if I weigh more than I think I "should?"

What can I do to lessen the significance of my weight?

If I am not a number on a scale, who am I?

Service

These are some ways I can be of help to other people:

_____

_____

_____

_____

_____

_____

_____

_____

_____

_____

_____

_____

_____

_____

_____

_____

_____

_____

_____

_____

_____

_____

"The best way to
FIND YOURSELF
is to lose yourself
IN THE SERVICE
OF OTHERS."
MAHATMA GHANDI

My Heart

"*Struggling*
means that you're fighting something,
that you're not just sitting there and
taking it or giving in."

ARIELLE LEE BLAIR

These are the ways I know I'm fighting:

_____

_____

_____

_____

_____

_____

_____

_____

_____

_____

_____

_____

_____

_____

_____

_____

_____

_____

_____

_____

_____

_____

_____

_____

_____

TRUE
HUNGER

Sometimes, what we are hungry for is not food.
Perhaps we crave security, acceptance, understanding,
friendship, intimacy, creativity, or even quiet time.

What am I hungry for today?

_____

_____

_____

_____

_____

_____

_____

_____

_____

_____

_____

_____

_____

_____

_____

_____

_____

INNER
WISDOM

"I have the courage to listen to my inner wisdom."

My Heart

50 THINGS THAT
I CELEBRATE ABOUT MYSELF

1. _____
2. _____
3. _____
4. _____
5. _____
6. _____
7. _____
8. _____
9. _____
10. _____
11. _____
12. _____
13. _____
14. _____
15. _____
16. _____
17. _____
18. _____
19. _____
20. _____

21. _____
22. _____
23. _____
24. _____
25. _____
26. _____
27. _____
28. _____
29. _____
30. _____
31. _____
32. _____
33. _____
34. _____
35. _____
36. _____
37. _____
38. _____
39. _____
40. _____
41. _____
42. _____
43. _____
44. _____
45. _____
46. _____
47. _____
48. _____
49. _____
50. _____

> "We're not meant to fit in.
> We're meant to
> STAND OUT."
>
> SARAH BAN
> BREATHNACH

My Heart

"And the day came
when the risk to remain
tight in the bud
was more painful than
the risk it took
to blossom."

ANAIS NIN

Today my only task, my only obligation,

is simply to listen to the whispers of my own heart.

My Heart

My
Body

"When you become more able to tune into your body and the signals it gives you, you begin to have more comfort and ease with having a physical form. You'll also notice that body sensations are often connected to emotions.

Be patient with yourself.

Body awareness takes time, and you are unfolding. Honor the process and honor yourself for making the effort."

MARY ANNE RITTER

BODY
dialogue

Our bodies thrive when we treat them as
valuable members of our team.

This is what my body would like to say to me:

_____

_____

_____

_____

_____

_____

_____

_____

_____

_____

_____

_____

_____

_____

_____

_____

_____

_____

_____

_____

_____

_____

_____

This is what I would like to say to my body:

_____
_____
_____
_____
_____
_____
_____
_____
_____
_____
_____
_____
_____
_____
_____
_____
_____
_____
_____
_____
_____
_____
_____
_____
_____
_____

My Heart

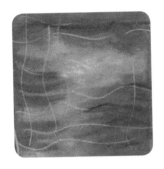

THIS IS HOW
MY BODY
LETS ME KNOW
I FEEL

TIRED:

HUNGRY:

HAPPY:

ANGRY:

SAD:

ANXIOUS:

"*Body Love*

doesn't mean
creating the perfect body;
rather it means living happily
in an imperfect one. "

RITA FREEDMAN

These are the reasons I am thankful for having a body:

_____

_____

_____

_____

_____

_____

_____

_____

_____

_____

_____

_____

_____

_____

_____

_____

_____

_____

_____

_____

_____

_____

_____

_____

_____

_____

OUR FAMILY TREE

We can usually find our body shape, size, and color on our family tree.

In my family, whose body looks like mine?

_____

_____

_____

_____

_____

_____

When did I first decide that there was something wrong with it?

_____

_____

_____

_____

_____

_____

_____

_____

_____

_____

What would happen if I accepted my body exactly as it is right here and right now?

human bodies

COME IN ALL SHAPES AND SIZES:
FAT, THIN, BOTH, NEITHER, AND
OTHERWISE.

This is how I would describe my body…using only positive terms:

"There is no wrong way
to have a
body."
GLENN MARLA

"*Most pleasures are small pleasures—*
a hot shower,
   a bowl of good soup,
      or a good book. "

MARY PIPHER

Here are the many small ways I can take care of my body:

Exercise

These are the ways I fit exercise into my life in a healthy way:

"Just as you might feel loved if
someone brought you flowers,
your body feels loved
when you use it."

ELIZABETH
"LILY" HILLS

Relaxation

When you begin to check in with yourself every day, you'll discover that sometimes what the body craves…is to slow down!

I honor my right to rest, rejuvenate, and relish my relaxation time.

TRANQUILITY

Here are my favorite mealtime

BLESSINGS AND PRAYERS
OF THANKSGIVING:

"BEFORE YOU TASTE
ANYTHING, RECITE A
blessing."
RABBI AKIVA

Mindful EATING

Today, I am going to observe what I eat without judgment.

Here are my reflections:

_____

_____

_____

_____

_____

_____

_____

_____

_____

_____

_____

_____

_____

_____

_____

_____

_____

_____

_____

THESE ARE THE FOODS
THAT I CAN EAT
WITHOUT FEAR
—AND WITH *pleasure!*

"Don't be afraid to
ENJOY YOUR FOOD."
EVELYN TRIBOLE &
ELYSE RESCH

ANIMAL CRACKERS
AND COCOA

to drink, that is still

the finest of suppers I think.

When I'm grown up and

can have what I please,

I think I shall always insist upon these."

CHRISTOPHER MORLEY

Today I will remember to be gentle with myself and celebrate the child within who needs and deserves delight in life.

My Recovery

*" Many
individuals who
have recovered from an eating
disorder consider their problems
with food and weight to have been their
greatest teachers, without which they might
not have seriously questioned their beliefs
and values, or faced their inner fears. They
learned to respond to old patterns in new
ways, enabling them to tackle other
problems with confidence
and compassion. "*

LINDSEY HALL

Checking In

"Checking in" will give you a better understanding of yourself and your ever-changing needs. Being able to recognize what is going on for you—emotionally, mentally, physically, and spiritually—leads to your being able to care for yourself in new ways that are nurturing, appropriate, and healthy.

GUIDELINES FOR CHECKING IN:

✔ Stop what you are doing and notice your breath.

✔ Become aware of any physical sensations, emotions, and racing thoughts without judgment.

✔ Ask, *What it is I need in this moment?*

TODAY I WILL WRITE
WHY MY RECOVERY IS
IMPORTANT
TO ME

_____

_____

_____

_____

_____

_____

_____

_____

_____

_____

_____

_____

_____

_____

_____

_____

_____

_____

_____

_____

_____

"To love one's self
IS THE BEGINNING
OF A LIFELONG ROMANCE."
OSCAR WILDE

AN EATING DISORDER

is sometimes the best way we know how to take care of ourselves in any given moment.

How has my ED taken care of me?

_____

_____

_____

_____

_____

_____

_____

_____

_____

_____

_____

_____

_____

_____

_____

_____

_____

_____

_____

In what other ways could I get those needs met?

_____

_____

_____

_____

_____

_____

_____

_____

_____

_____

_____

_____

_____

_____

_____

_____

_____

_____

_____

_____

_____

_____

_____

_____

Celebrate

I celebrate my greatest victories
thus far in my recovery.

I record them here as a reminder of how far I've come.

_____

_____

_____

_____

_____

_____

_____

_____

_____

_____

_____

_____

_____

_____

_____

_____

_____

_____

_____

"RECOVERY
is a
MARATHON,
not a sprint."

JENNI
SCHAEFER

Conversation with ED

Your eating disorder has a voice of its own, which is different than the voice of your healthy self. What might they say to each other?

The voice of Ed:

_____

_____

_____

_____

_____

_____

_____

_____

_____

_____

_____

_____

_____

_____

_____

_____

_____

_____

_____

_____

_____

_____

The voice of my healthy self:

_____

_____

_____

_____

_____

_____

_____

_____

_____

_____

_____

_____

_____

_____

_____

_____

_____

_____

_____

_____

_____

_____

_____

_____

_____

Planning AHEAD

The secret to managing triggers effectively is not to avoid them, but rather to know what they are, catch yourself in the moment, and have a plan of action.

Here is one of my most common triggers, and a step-by-step plan for handling it in a proactive, positive way:

_____
_____
_____
_____
_____
_____
_____
_____
_____
_____
_____
_____
_____
_____
_____
_____
_____
_____
_____

"True Life
is lived when tiny changes occur."
LEO TOLSTOY

I will be true to myself today.

Self-love

CAN BE DELICIOUS.

Life
AFTER ED

Imagining what life might be like without an eating disorder connects you to the idea that you have a future—and it's a good one.

These are my fantasies about life after Ed:

_____

_____

_____

_____

_____

_____

_____

_____

_____

_____

_____

_____

_____

_____

_____

_____

_____

_____

_____

_____

_____

_____

"Knowing

—without doing what's required for growth—
is an empty insight.

'DO THE KNOW'

means taking the actual steps towards change:
doing something different,
adding a healthy habit, risking love,
writing a new soundtrack for your life. "

BETH HARTMAN MCGILLEY

I will take recovery action today in this way:

_____

_____

_____

_____

_____

_____

_____

_____

_____

_____

_____

_____

_____

_____

_____

_____

_____

_____

_____

_____

_____

_____

_____

_____

COPING
SKILLS

My personal list of things I know how to do when things get to be too much and
I don't want to revert to old behaviors:

_____

_____

_____

_____

_____

_____

_____

_____

_____

_____

_____

_____

_____

_____

_____

_____

_____

_____

_____

_____

I can courageously handle anything with ease and intelligence as long as I take it one moment at a time.

1

LESSONS
in Disguise

Setbacks are a normal and natural part of the recovery journey, and the way you frame them can make all the difference. How about lessons in disguise?

Try this approach: if a setback happened to your best friend, what would you say to him/her?

_____

_____

_____

_____

_____

_____

_____

_____

_____

_____

_____

_____

_____

_____

_____

_____

_____

_____

_____

_____

_____

_____

_____

_____

_____

_____

_____

_____

_____

_____

_____

_____

_____

_____

_____

_____

_____

> "LIFE IS _just one damned thing after another._"
>
> FRANK WARD
> O'MALLEY

_____

_____

_____

_____

_____

_____

My Recovery

"There is no right way;
there are only starting points.
And from there, where we arrive
is as individual, unique and
precious as we are."

ANONYMOUS